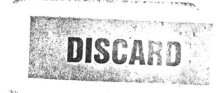

D1372489

Rhinoceroses

Ethan Grucella

Please visit our Web site, www.garethstevens.com. For a free color catalog of all our high-quality books, call toll free 1-800-542-2595 or fax 1-877-542-2596.

Library of Congress Cataloging-in-Publication Data

Grucella, Ethan.
 Rhinoceroses / Ethan Grucella.
   p. cm. – (Animals that live in the grasslands)
 Includes index.
 ISBN 978-1-4339-3882-5 (pbk.)
 ISBN 978-1-4339-3883-2 (6-pack)
 ISBN 978-1-4339-3881-8 (library binding)
 1. Rhinoceroses—Juvenile literature. I. Title.
 QL737.U63G79 2011
 599.66'8–dc22

                                        2010012718

First Edition

Published in 2011 by
Gareth Stevens Publishing
111 East 14th Street, Suite 349
New York, NY 10003

Designer: Michael J. Flynn
Editor: Therese Shea

Photo credits: Cover, pp. 1, 5, 7, 9 (both), 11 (both), 13, 15, 17, 19, 21, back cover Shutterstock.com.

Printed in the United States of America

CPSIA compliance information: Batch #CS10GS: For further information contact Gareth Stevens, New York, New York at 1-800-542-2595.

Table of Contents

Boldface words appear in the glossary.

African Rhinos

Two kinds of rhinoceroses live in Africa. Black rhinos live mainly in wooded areas. White rhinos live in the **grasslands**. Both are really gray!

An African rhino has two horns on its nose. The horns are very hard. The rhino uses them when it **attacks**.

horns

Black rhinos are sometimes called "hook lipped." White rhinos are sometimes called "square lipped." Can you see the difference?

black rhino

white rhino

The shape of a black rhino's mouth helps it pick leaves off bushes and trees. The shape of a white rhino's mouth helps it eat grass.

black rhino

white rhino

11

Rhinos like to hide from the hot African sun. They lie in shady places. They also take mud baths!

Talking Rhinos

Rhinos talk to each other by making noises that people can't hear! They also growl, grunt, squeak, and snort.

A rhinoceros snorts before it **charges** at an animal. It runs very fast. If it misses, it may turn and try again. Rhinos are known for being grumpy!

Friends and Enemies

Some birds sit on rhinos and eat bugs off them. The birds make noise if they see danger. The noise warns the rhino.

People are rhinos' greatest enemies. Rhinos are hunted for their horns. They almost became **extinct**. There are now laws to keep rhinos safe.

Fast Facts

Height	up to 6 feet (1.8 meters) at the shoulder
Length	up to 13 feet (4 meters) from head to rear; tail is up to 27.5 inches (70 centimeters)
Weight	up to 5,000 pounds (2,270 kilograms)
Diet	black rhino: leaves, fruit white rhino: grass
Average life span	up to 40 years

Glossary

attack: to try to harm

charge: to attack by rushing forward

extinct: having died out so there are no animals of that kind

grasslands: land on which grass is the main kind of plant life

For More Information

Books

Murray, Peter. *Rhinos.* Chanhassen, MN: Child's World, 2006.

Orme, Helen. *Rhinos in Danger.* New York, NY: Bearport Publishing, 2007.

Pohl, Kathleen. *Rhinos.* Milwaukee, WI: Weekly Reader Publishing, 2008.

Web Sites

Rhinoceros
www.awf.org/content/wildlife/detail/rhinoceros
Read more about black and white rhinos and see video of them in action.

White Rhinoceroses
animals.nationalgeographic.com/animals/mammals/ white-rhinoceros
Read about white rhinos and see a map that shows where they roam in Africa.

Index

About the Author

Though a practicing physician like his parents, Ethan Grucella is an amateur zoologist with an enthusiasm for African animals. He lives in Cleveland, Ohio, where he writes wildlife books in his spare time.